This book belongs to:

_____

MY FIRST
Piano
Lessons

FUN, EASY-TO-FOLLOW
INSTRUCTIONS FOR KIDS

Emily Norris

Illustrated by Malgorzata Detner

Z Kids • New York

To my students (past, present, and future)

and the grown-ups in their lives.

You took the initiative to try piano lessons.

You embraced my creative teaching.

You trusted the process.

And now you play the piano!

From the bottom of my heart, thank you!

Enjoy making music for life.

All rights reserved.
Published in the United States by Z Kids, an imprint of Zeitgeist™,
a division of Penguin Random House LLC, New York.
zeitgeistpublishing.com

Zeitgeist™ is a trademark of Penguin Random House LLC
ISBN: 9780593435809
Ebook ISBN: 9780593690246

Illustrations by Malgorzata Detner
Book design by Katy Brown
Author photograph © by Haylee Beth Photography
Illustrator photograph © by MDetner
Edited by Ada Fung

Printed in the United States of America
3rd Printing

CONTENTS

Introduction

Hi!

My name is G-sharp the Giraffe,
and I am so excited to meet you!

I am a giraffe who loves music. See?
One of my spots is a musical note!

We are going on a journey to learn your first
10 songs on the piano!

Don't worry! You will not go on this journey alone.
I am here to help you! I will teach you new
things to help you play every song.

Remember that:

Journeys can be tiring. So take breaks!

Journeys can be hard. It's okay to make mistakes!

Journeys are exciting. So let's have fun!

Journeys start off slow and easy. We don't want to move too fast at the beginning. So I will teach you the first songs using numbers, because those are easy! As our journey continues, you'll be learning new musical symbols and the songs will start to look more like real sheet music. By the end, you will be reading music like a champ!

How to Use This Book

I will be helping you, so look for me on the pages!

Each lesson will begin with me teaching you new things about music and the piano. I will even share fun facts about music along the way!

Then we will play a song! You've probably heard a lot of the songs in this book. But you might notice that I changed some of the lyrics. This is so the words match the notes that you are learning! At the top of your sheet music, you will see an image like this one, which tells you where to put your hands for the song.

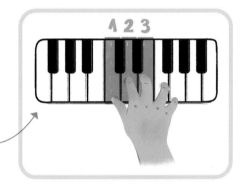

And look out for me on your sheet music! I will be around to point out things to watch for as you play.

When you get to the end, you will see Your Trusty Piano Guidebook (page 44). Here is where I will put the new music words we will learn! You can head there whenever you're not sure what a music word means.

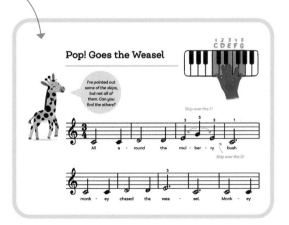

Before You Play

We have to prepare! Our journey will be so much more fun if we do. So follow me! Let's do some activities together.

How Should I Sit?

Giraffes do not sit very much. But sitting is important for playing piano!

Sit near the front of your bench, and make your back as straight as my neck. Can't reach the floor? You might need a footstool to support your feet. This helps you stay relaxed and keeps you from leaning too far forward.

Where Do I Put My Hands?

Make two fists and put your arms straight out.

Are your hands right above the black keys? Then you are at the right distance from your seat to the keys. If they are not, scoot your bench back or forward a little until your hands are right above the black keys.

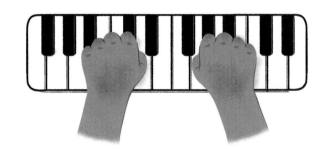

What Are the Keys, Anyway?

Piano keys are the white and black shapes on your piano. The white keys are called naturals, and the black keys are called sharps and flats. You press them down to make a sound. You can play 1 key at a time or a lot of them all at once.

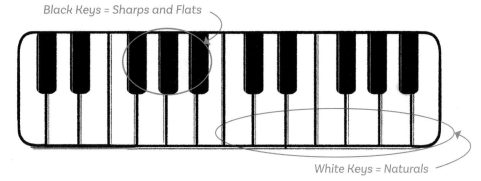

Black Keys = Sharps and Flats

White Keys = Naturals

Let's try playing some keys! Put your pointer finger of your right hand on the keyboard, on any white key. Let's play 1 key at a time moving to your right. What do you hear? That's right—the notes get higher and higher. This means you are moving "up" the piano!

Now put your pointer finger of your left hand on any white key and play 1 key at a time, moving your finger to your left. The notes get lower and lower, right? You're moving "down" the piano.

On our piano journey, we will only be playing the white keys. But you can still make music with the black keys. Give it a try!

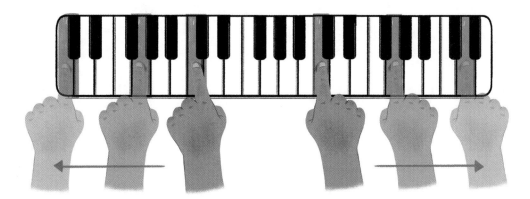

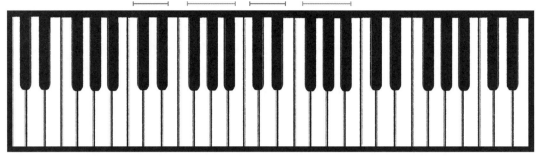

What's Middle C?

Some keyboards have 61 keys and others have 76. But did you know that pianos have 88 keys? Wow! I don't even have that many spots!

On the piano, there are two kinds of black-key groups: a "2-group" and a "3-group."

Find a "2-group" of black keys near the middle of the piano. See the white key under the first black key? This key is a C. Can you guess what the C in the middle of the piano is called? That's right! It's **middle C**. Middle C is important to know because it is the starting point to help us find the other keys on the piano.

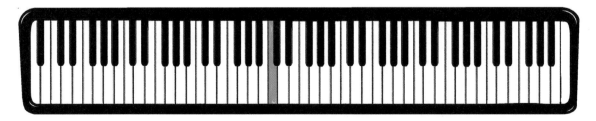

Middle C

How Do I Hold My Hands?

Pretend that you are picking up a pretty rock, with your fingers curved around the top of the rock. Now put your hands on the piano keys, keeping your fingers curved, as if the rock is still there. Now you have the perfect hand shape for playing piano!

Where Do I Put My Fingers?

Your fingers are used to play the piano, so they're pretty important! Each finger has its own number. This is so you can see which finger goes on which key on the piano. Hold your hands up just like this picture, and let's count!

Remember, your thumb is number 1!

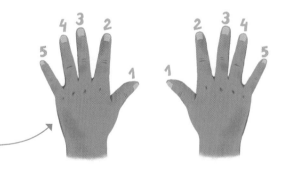

In this book, we'll use your right hand to play most of the songs! Your right-hand thumb will almost always rest on middle C. Can you match the fingers on your right hand with the correct keys in the picture on the right?

Don't worry about your left hand! Rest it lightly on the keys. We will use it later.

Now you're ready to learn your first 10 songs!

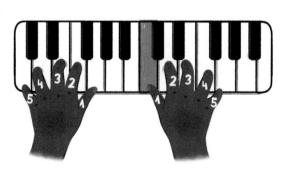

Sticky Fingers

SONG
Hot Cross Buns

WHAT YOU'LL LEARN

- Quarter note
- Half note
- Finger numbers

Giraffes spend most of their day eating, and I'm already hungry! So let's start our piano journey by learning the song "Hot Cross Buns." It's an easy song about one of my favorite snacks! Ready to get those fingers sticky?

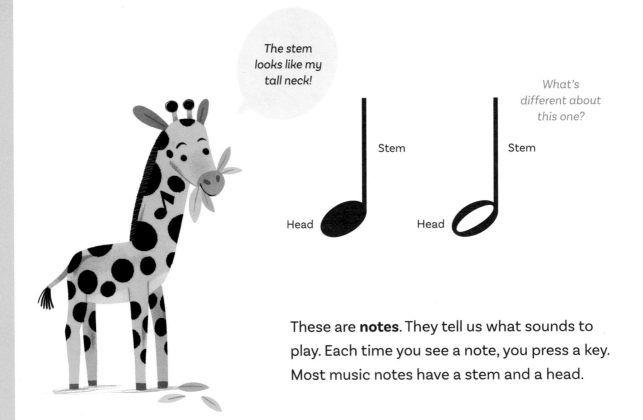

The stem looks like my tall neck!

What's different about this one?

Stem

Stem

Head

Head

These are **notes**. They tell us what sounds to play. Each time you see a note, you press a key. Most music notes have a stem and a head.

1
"quick"

1
"quick"

1
"quick"

1
"quick"

These are **quarter notes**. It means to play for 1 beat. A **beat** is a way of measuring how long to hold down a key. When you see a quarter note, say the word "quick" each time you press a key. Try it with any key!

These are **half notes**. It means to play for 2 beats. When you see one, say the words "half note" each time you press a key. Your finger "sticks" to the note longer. Give it a try!

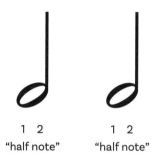

1 2
"half note"

1 2
"half note"

We're almost ready to play our first song! You will see the hand position above the sheet music. The numbers above the notes are the finger numbers. Press that finger down to play the correct key.

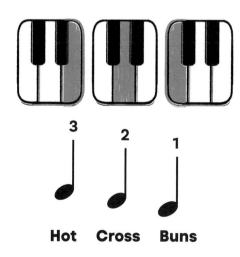

3   2   1

Hot   Cross   Buns

Hot Cross Buns

Begin here

3   2   1   3   2   1

Hot   cross   buns,   hot   cross   buns.

Go to the next line!

3   3   2   2   3   2   1

One,   two,   three,   four,   hot   cross   buns.

*This symbol is the **double bar**. It means it's the end of the song.*

FUN FACT

Pianos have been around for over 350 years! Did you know that the black and white keys on the first pianos used to be REVERSED? The black keys were white, and the white keys were black. Why? Nobody really knows..

Treble Clef and Long Notes

SONG
Alouette

WHAT YOU'LL LEARN
- Treble clef
- Dotted half note
- Whole note

Giraffes live in Africa, and we don't get to visit other places very often. So let's visit France and learn a song in a new language. This song is called "Alouette," and it means "lark." A lark is a bird with beautiful feathers. This song uses the same 3 keys from our last song. But we will add some long notes.

First, I'd like you to meet the **treble clef!** It is a symbol at the beginning of your sheet music. It means to play keys middle C and higher. When we see a treble clef, that means we should play with our right hand.

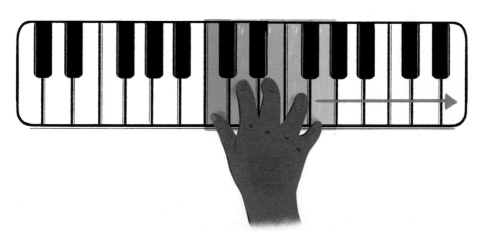

Now let's learn the long notes!

This is a **dotted half note**. It means to play for 3 beats. It's just a half note with a dot. Say "half note dot" each time you press a key. Your finger "sticks" to the key a little longer than it would for the half note. Give it a try! Next, try playing a dotted half note, then a quarter note right after it. Can you hear the difference?

1 2 3
"half note dot"

This is a **whole note**. It means to play for 4 beats. This is the longest note! Say "whole note long-est" each time you press a key. Try it with any key!

1 2 3 4
"whole note long-est"

FUN FACT

Different countries have different names for the notes that we learned today. In Great Britain, they call a quarter note a "crochet" (pronounced "cro-shay") because it looks like the hook you use to crochet, a form of weaving where you loop and connect yarn or thread together to make everything from blankets and scarves to stuffed animals and even baskets!

Alouette

Remember, treble clef = playing with your right hand!

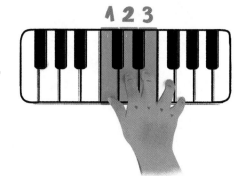

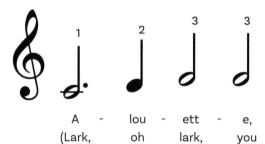

A - lou - ett - e, gen-tille a - lou - ette.
(Lark, oh lark, you nice and friend-ly lark.)

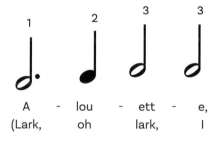

A - lou - ett - e, j'aime beau-coup tes plumes.
(Lark, oh lark, I love your fair fea - thers.)

A Natural Name

SONGS

- **Mary Had a Little Lamb**
- **Freddy Had a Puppy Dog**
- **Gary Had a Tall Giraffe**

WHAT YOU'LL LEARN

- **Names of the natural (white) keys**

Did you know that giraffes and lambs are cousins? We both have hooves and an even number of toes on each foot! Let's visit my cousin and learn the song "Mary Had a Little Lamb." This song uses 4 keys and they each have a name. Let's learn them together!

A **key name** is the capital letter for each piano key. In this lesson, we're going to learn the key names for each natural key—those are the white ones!

Let's start at middle C, the first white key below the two-group of black keys in the middle of the piano. This is where you've been resting your thumb so far!

The next two white keys are D and E, just like in the alphabet.

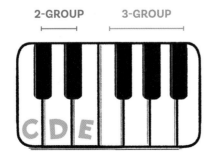

Now let's go to the white keys under the 3 black keys. The first two are F and G, just like you'd expect. Then we go back to the beginning of the alphabet with A and B.

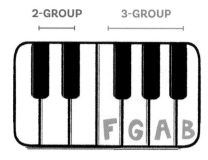

And because the piano is a repeat pattern, right after that it's back to C!

Here's the full set of natural key names:

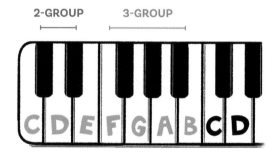

From now on, you will see a letter instead of a finger number in the sheet music. So, when you see the letter E in the note, you'll press the E key. But don't worry, you will still see some finger numbers, to help you remember which note to play.

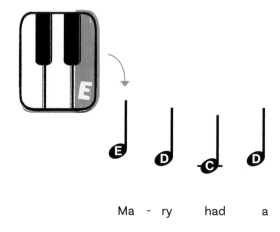

Ma - ry   had   a

Mary Had a Little Lamb

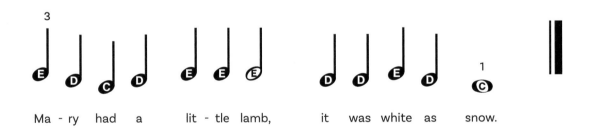

Freddy Had a Puppy Dog

Are you up for a challenge? Let's change up your hand position to play a different version of "Mary Had a Little Lamb"—"Freddy Had a Puppy Dog"!

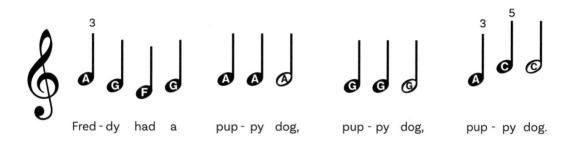

Fred - dy   had   a   pup - py   dog,   pup - py   dog,   pup - py   dog.

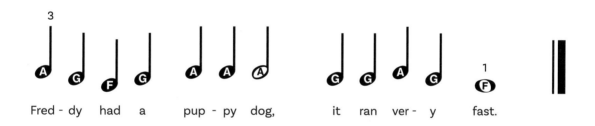

Fred - dy   had   a   pup - py   dog,   it   ran   ver - y   fast.

FUN FACT

Some countries, like the United States and Canada, use letters for the key names. Just like we did in this lesson! But other countries, like China and Japan, use words. Instead of C-D-E, they use Do-Re-Mi. There's even a song to help remember those words. It's from a musical, *The Sound of Music*. Have you heard it?

Gary Had a Tall Giraffe

Should we switch it up one more time?
This version is called "Gary Had a Tall Giraffe"—
because your hand starts on the G note!

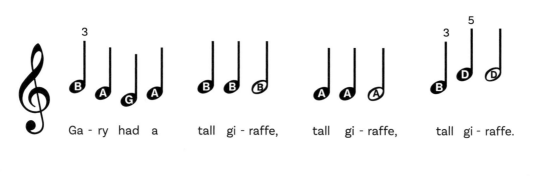

Ga - ry had a   tall gi - raffe,   tall gi - raffe,   tall gi - raffe.

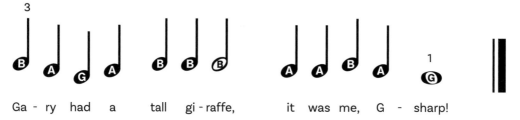

Ga - ry had a   tall gi - raffe,   it was me, G - sharp!

Guiding Lights

SONG
Brother John

WHAT YOU'LL LEARN

- **Guide notes (middle C and G)**

Look! There's a cave up ahead. We'll need a guide to help us explore this new place—just like certain music notes serve as guides on the music staff.

The **staff** is a group of 5 lines and 4 spaces. Each line and space is home to a music note—and a key on the piano.

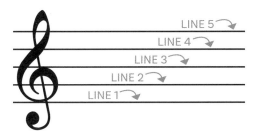

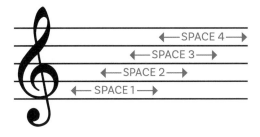

A **line note** has a line going through the middle of its head.

A **space note** sits in a space.

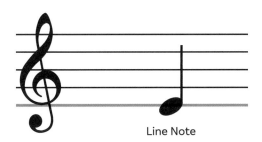

Line Note

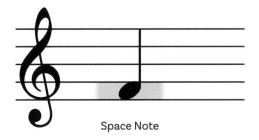

Space Note

The 2 **guide notes** on the treble staff are middle C and G. Guide notes are important notes that you can memorize so that you can find other notes around them more easily. Middle C and G are both line notes.

Middle C lives on a **ledger line**, which is an extra line that isn't on the staff. You can think of it as a special "cat whisker" just for middle C. G lives on the second line of the staff.

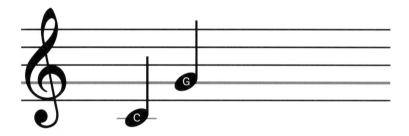

Because we just learned where middle C and G sit on the staff, you won't see those letters for the notes in this song. The more notes we learn, the fewer letters we'll see. But you will still see some finger numbers. Let the finger numbers, middle C, and G be your guiding lights through our song!

FUN FACT
There was a famous German music composer named Beethoven. When he was 44 years old, he lost his hearing. He had to lay his head on top of the piano to feel the vibrations. That was his way of hearing the music! Can you feel vibrations on YOUR piano?

Brother John

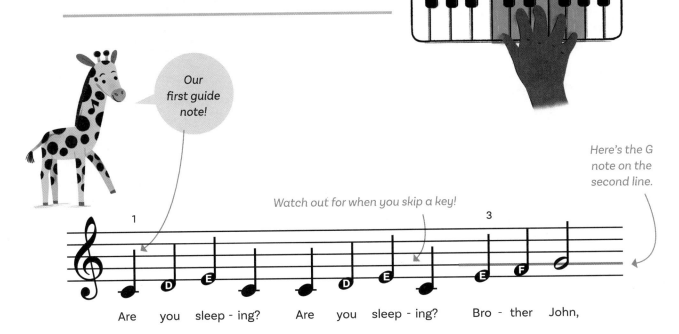

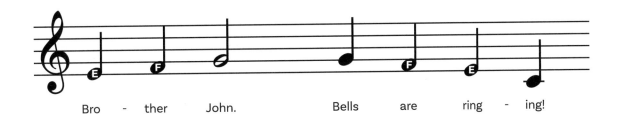

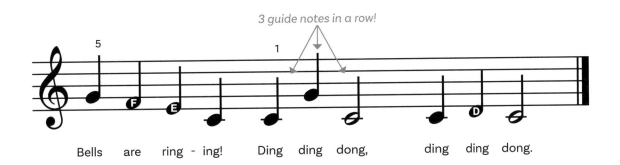

A Tangled Web

SONG
Itsy Bitsy Spider

WHAT YOU'LL LEARN
- **Bar lines**
- **4/4 time signature**

Sometimes reading music can be confusing—a little bit like getting tangled up in a spiderweb. Learning how music is organized on the page will save us from that sticky, tangly fate!

Music is organized by **measures**. A measure is a group of notes with a certain number of beats. Think of it as a house for your notes!

Measure

Just like many houses have a front door and a back door, measures have **bar lines**, which are lines that show the beginning and end of a measure.

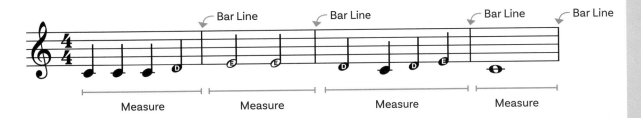

The number right after the treble clef also helps us read and understand music. It's called a **time signature**. A time signature has a top and bottom number, and it tells us about the beats in the song.

The top number tells how many beats are in each measure. In this song, the top number is 4, so each measure has 4 beats. The bottom number tells us which note gets 1 beat. If the bottom number is 4, the quarter note gets 1 beat. We already learned that! We call this a 4/4 ("four-four") time signature.

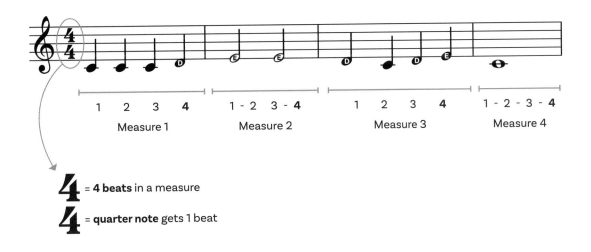

Itsy Bitsy Spider

How many beats are there in each measure?

How many measures are in this song?

Watch out for when you skip a key!

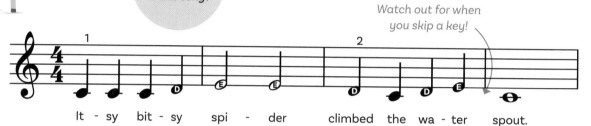

It – sy   bit – sy   spi   –   der   climbed   the   wa – ter   spout.

Down   came   the   rain   and   washed   the   spi – der   out.

How long should you play this key?

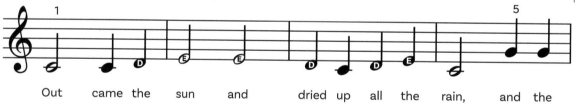

Out   came   the   sun   and   dried   up   all   the   rain,   and   the

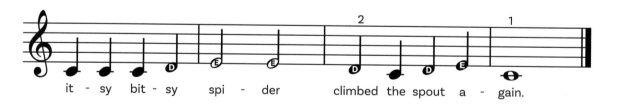

it – sy   bit – sy   spi   –   der   climbed   the   spout   a   –   gain.

Pop On Over

SONG

Pop! Goes the Weasel

WHAT YOU'LL LEARN

- **Steps**
- **Skips**
- **3/4 time signature**

Watch out! Weasels sometimes pop their heads out of the ground and make holes. Let's step carefully and skip over the holes so we don't disturb them. We can also step and skip on the piano. Pop on over and take a look!

A **step** is the next key up or down on the piano. It moves from a line to the next space (like middle C to D), or from a space to the next line (like F to E).

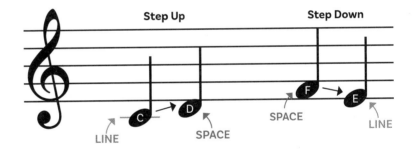

A **skip** is when you skip a key up or down the piano. It moves from a space to the next space (like D to F), or from a line to the next line (like G to E).

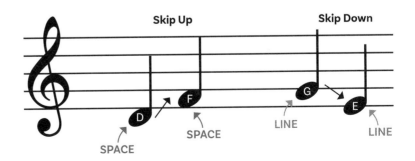

In the last lesson, we learned about time signatures. The time signature for "Pop! Goes the Weasel" has a 3 as the top number. That means there are only 3 beats in each measure. We call this a 3/4 ("three-four") time signature.

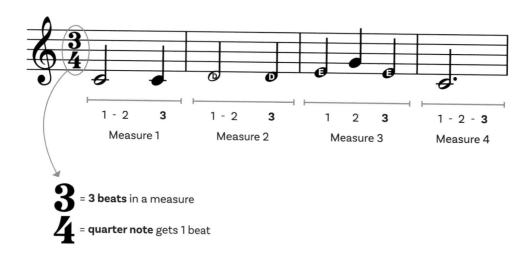

3 = **3 beats** in a measure

4 = **quarter note** gets 1 beat

Now it's time to learn "Pop! Goes the Weasel"! Can you step and skip in the right places? Don't worry, I'll be there to help you.

Pop! Goes the Weasel

I've pointed out some of the skips, but not all of them. Can you find the others?

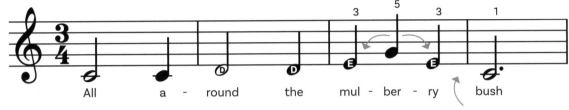

Skip over the F!

Skip over the D!

All — a - round — the — mul - ber - ry — bush

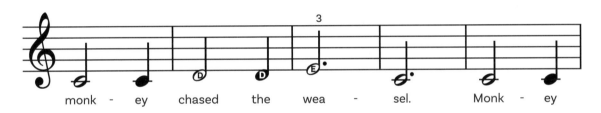

monk - ey — chased — the — wea — sel. — Monk — ey

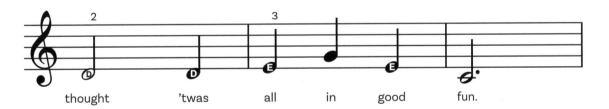

thought — 'twas — all — in — good — fun.

Another skip!

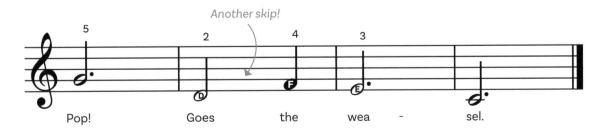

Pop! — Goes — the — wea — sel.

Tiptoe, Tiptoe

SONG
The Farmer in the Dell

WHAT YOU'LL LEARN
- 8th notes
- D, E, and F notes

Shh! I think I see a farmer with his cows over there. We don't want to disturb them, so let's tiptoe quickly around the field. While we do that, let's learn how to play a new song and "tiptoe" with our fingers!

This is an **8th note**. It means to play for half of a beat. You will usually see two 8th notes connected together by a horizontal line. These are called beamed 8th notes.

Beamed 8th Notes

= ½

½ + ½ = 1

When you see beamed 8th notes, say the word "tiptoe" as you play them. You'll notice that your finger does not stick to the key very long!

½   ½
"Tip - toe"

½   ½
"Tip - toe"

Now let's learn where the D, E, and F sit on the staff! They are the 3 notes in between middle C and G.

D and F live in spaces. D is dangling below the staff. F is just one hop down from G. E lives on the line between D and F.

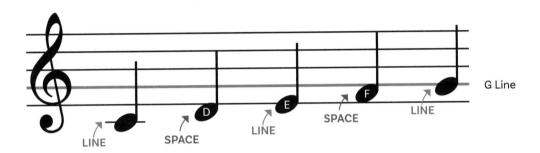

Since we learned 3 new notes, you'll notice that there are fewer letters in this song! Don't worry, you will still see some finger numbers to help guide you.

FUN FACT

Just like your bicycle, a piano has pedals! When you press a piano pedal down with your foot, it changes the sound. But on the really old pianos, you didn't use your foot! You had to use your hands instead. And on some pianos, you had to use your knees. If you have pedals, try them while playing "The Farmer in the Dell"! What differences in sound do you hear?

The Farmer in the Dell

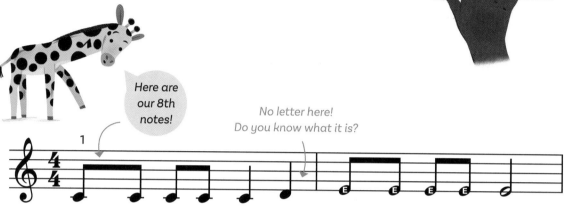

1. Far - mer in the dell, the far - mer in the dell.
2. Far - mer feeds the cat, the far - mer feeds the cat.
3. Cat chas - es the mouse, the cat chas - es the mouse.
4. Mouse takes all the cheese, the mouse takes all the cheese.
5. Cheese stands all a - lone, the cheese stands all a - lone.

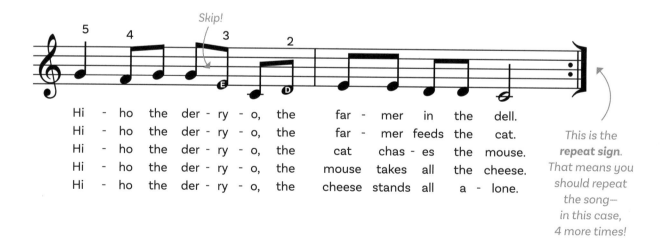

Hi - ho the der - ry - o, the far - mer in the dell.
Hi - ho the der - ry - o, the far - mer feeds the cat.
Hi - ho the der - ry - o, the cat chas - es the mouse.
Hi - ho the der - ry - o, the mouse takes all the cheese.
Hi - ho the der - ry - o, the cheese stands all a - lone.

A New Friend, Bass Clef

SONG
The Wheels on the Bus

WHAT YOU'LL LEARN

- Bass clef
- Left-hand finger numbers

Whew! We tiptoed past the cows and made it to the highway. My hooves are tired, so let's stop walking and catch the bus.

The **bass clef** is another symbol at the beginning of music, just like the treble clef. When you see the bass clef, it means you should play keys middle C and lower, using your left hand.

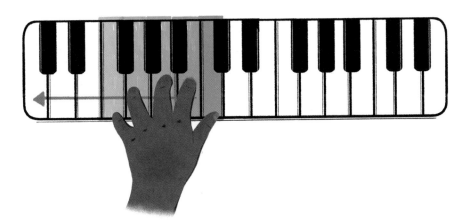

The **grand staff** is a combination of both the treble staff and the bass staff, connected with a bracket. This is how all piano music is written!

The stems on the notes in the bass staff go down instead of up. But the notes still get the same number of beats.

Grand Staff

Since this will be our first time using our left hand, let's refresh our memory on the finger numbers. Remember, your thumb is number 1, the next finger is number 2, your middle finger is number 3, then comes number 4, and finally, your pinkie finger is number 5.

From now on, both of your hands will be on the piano at the same time! Don't worry, this song includes finger numbers to help you!

The Wheels on the Bus

This song uses a lot of skips!

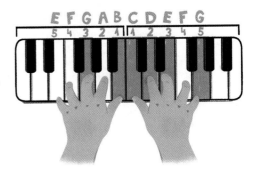

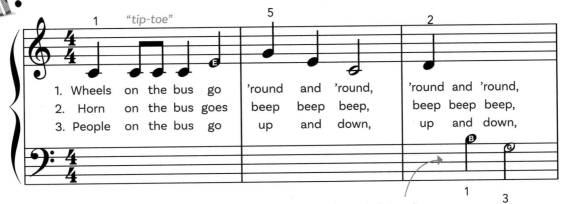

1. "tip-toe"   **5**   **2**

1. Wheels on the bus go 'round and 'round, 'round and 'round,
2. Horn on the bus goes beep beep beep, beep beep beep,
3. People on the bus go up and down, up and down,

Time to play with your left hand!

1   **3**

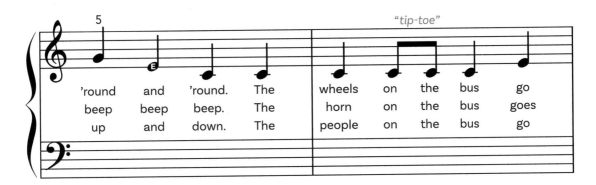

5   "tip-toe"

'round and 'round. The wheels on the bus go
beep beep beep. The horn on the bus goes
up and down. The people on the bus go

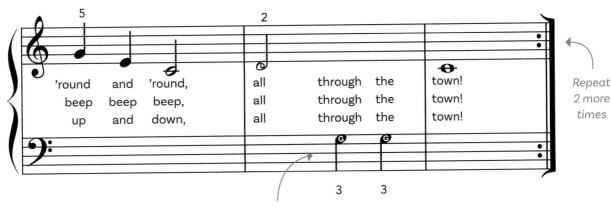

5   **2**

'round and 'round, all through the town!
beep beep beep, all through the town!
up and down, all through the town!

Repeat 2 more times

3   **3**

Here's that left hand again!

Low Bridge, Everybody Down

SONG
London Bridge

WHAT YOU'LL LEARN
- **F, G, A, and B notes in bass staff**
- **Dynamics**

Look! We're in England and I see London Bridge. But my neck is sticking out of the top of the bus. I'll need to duck down. Let's learn how to read some more notes in the bass staff so we can get low and make it under this bridge!

Remember the bass staff? It has 5 lines and 4 spaces for notes, just like the treble staff.

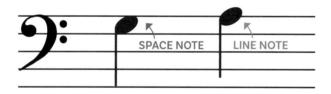

The guide note on the bass staff is F, which sits on the second line between the bass clef's 2 dots. This note will help you find other notes in the bass staff!

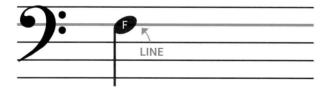

G and B on the bass staff live in spaces. G is just a step up from F, and B is the boss, sitting on top! A is the first letter in the alphabet, so it sits on the first line.

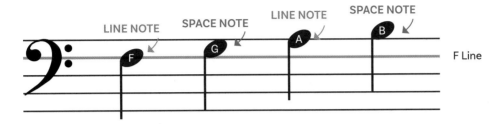

Wait! Before we jump right into playing "London Bridge," let's talk about the "*p*" and "*f*" you will see at the beginning of the sheet music. These are called **dynamics**, which tell you how loud or soft to play the verse.

The "*p*" stands for "**piano**," which means "soft." When you see a "*p*," press each key in that verse lightly to make a soft sound.

The "*f*" stands for "**forte**," which means "loud." When you see an "*f*," press each key in that verse harder to make a loud sound.

f Forte = Loud

p Piano = Soft

London Bridge

Pay attention to
your dynamics!

f
p
f
p

1. Lon - don Bridge is | fall - ing down, | fall - ing down,
2. Build it up with | i - ron bars, | i - ron bars,
3. I - ron bars will | bend and break, | bend and break,
4. Lon - don Bridge is | fall - ing down, | fall - ing down,

Which hand do you use here?

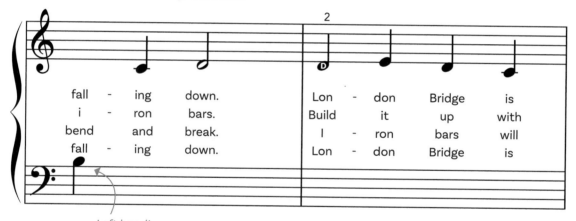

fall - ing down. | Lon - don Bridge is
i - ron bars. | Build it up with
bend and break. | I - ron bars will
fall - ing down. | Lon - don Bridge is

Left hand!

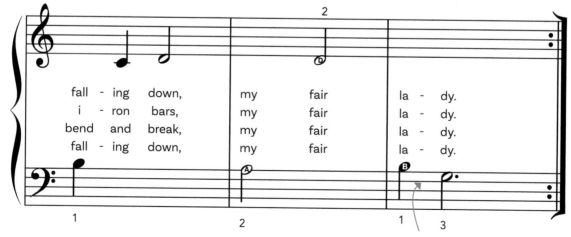

fall - ing down, | my fair | la - dy.
i - ron bars, | my fair | la - dy.
bend and break, | my fair | la - dy.
fall - ing down, | my fair | la - dy.

*Repeat
3 more
times!*

Step or skip?

Both Hands In

SONG
Lightly Row

WHAT YOU'LL LEARN
- Bass C
- Hands-together playing

We made it under the bridge. Now it's time to grab our little boat and row away across the ocean! We need to play with both hands at the same time for this song!

But before we play, let's learn one more note in the bass staff. This time, using whole notes!

This is bass C. It lives in the third space on the bass staff. Just count the spaces from the top down and say the rhyme: "1-2-3, there is C!"

FUN FACT

Did you know that the piano's real name is "pianoforte"? That makes sense because the piano plays both soft and loud! We gave it the nickname "piano" because "pianoforte" is just too long. Do you have a nickname, too?

Remember when we learned middle C in the treble staff? Bass C is a lower C on the piano.

In our other songs, our right and left hands took turns playing the notes. But this song is special! We will learn **hands-together playing**. This is when you play notes with both hands at the same time!

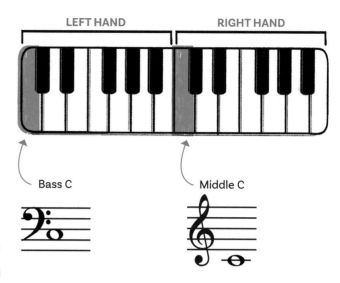

LEFT HAND   RIGHT HAND

Bass C   Middle C

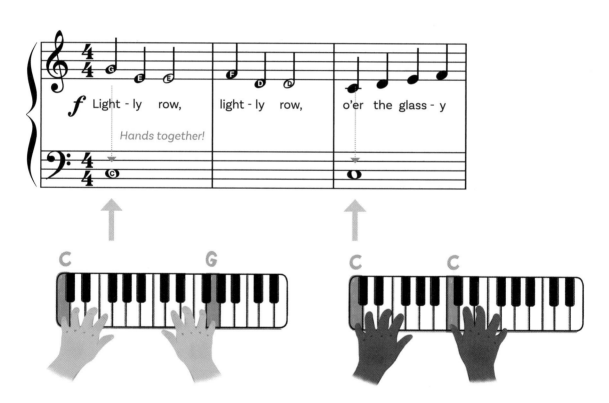

f Light - ly   row,   light - ly   row,   o'er   the   glass - y

Hands together!

C   G   C   C

You'll know when to play the notes at the same time because they'll be directly above and below each other. This creates harmony. Harmony is when different notes are heard at the same time. It's so beautiful. Have fun playing our last song!

Lightly Row

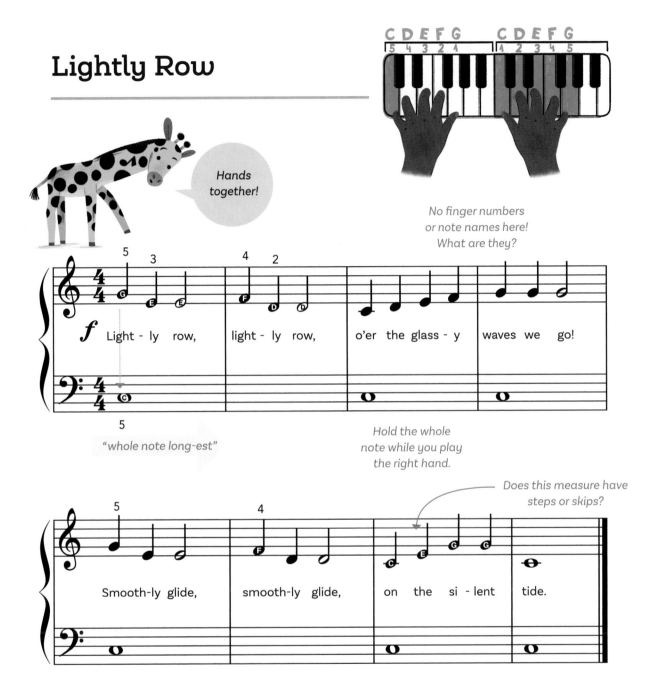

FUN FACT

The piano is special. It's one of the only instruments that plays in 2 staffs—treble and bass! Other instruments, like the violin, the guitar, and even your voice, use just 1 staff.

Your Trusty Piano Guidebook

Here are all the new words we learned on our journey!

8th note: Hold for a half beat; two together are beamed 8th notes

bar line: A straight line that shows the beginning and end of a measure

bass clef: A symbol at the beginning of music to show the low notes

beat: A way of measuring how long to hold down a key

dotted half note: Hold for 3 beats

double bar: A symbol that means the end of the song

dynamics: How loud or soft to play a note

forte (*f*): Loud

grand staff: Treble and bass staffs together with a bracket connecting them

guide note: An important note whose location on the staff you can memorize to find other notes around it more easily (*examples: middle C, treble G, and bass F*)

half note: Hold for 2 beats

hands-together playing: Playing with both hands at the same time

key name: A capital letter for each key

ledger line: An extra line that's not on the staff (middle C has a ledger line!)

line note: A note that has a line going through its head

measure: A group of notes with a certain number of beats

middle C: The C in the middle of the piano

note: A symbol with a head and a stem

piano (p): Soft

quarter note: Hold for 1 beat

repeat sign: A symbol that means to repeat the song

skip: When you skip a key up or down on the piano

space note: A note that sits in a space between lines

staff: A group of 5 lines and 4 spaces

step: The next key up or down on the piano

time signature: Two numbers that tell us about the beats in the song (*examples: 4/4 and 3/4*)

treble clef: A symbol at the beginning of music to show the high notes

whole note: Hold for 4 beats

Certificate of Completion

You did it!

_____

NAME

HAS COMPLETED THEIR FIRST
10 SONGS ON THE PIANO!

EVEN THOUGH THIS JOURNEY WAS SHORT,
YOUR LOVE OF MUSIC WILL LAST A LIFETIME.
ENJOY PLAYING PIANO!

_____

DATE

Resources

Excited to keep learning piano? Here are some books and videos to continue your journey!

Videos

Parents, you can find these resources on YouTube:

EBN Music with Emily Norris
youtube.com/@ebnmusic

Hoffman Academy
youtube.com/c/HoffmanAcademy

My Music Workshop
youtube.com/c/MyMusicWorkshop

Pocket Tutorials for Music
youtube.com/c/PocketTutorialsforMusic

Books

My First Piano Adventure for the Young Beginner (Nancy and Randall Faber, 2006)

WunderKeys Primer books (Andrea and Trevor Dow, 2017)

About the Author

Emily Norris has been through her own musical journey!

At age 7, she used her dad's turntable and listened to Bee Gees and Pet Shop Boys records on repeat.

At age 10, she started piano lessons in Tupelo, Mississippi, playing through the whole book in two lessons.

At age 15, she became the music director and piano accompanist for a children's production of *The Wizard of Oz* in Trenton, Tennessee.

At age 22, she taught piano and voice lessons in Clarksville, Tennessee, while also teaching 5th grade.

At age 33, she started her own piano and voice studio in the middle of a global pandemic.

And now, just like G-sharp, she takes young students on their own journeys to learn, love, and enjoy piano!

On days off, she'll go on journeys with her husband on the back of his Honda Shadow motorcycle, still listening to Bee Gees and Pet Shop Boys "records" on repeat.

Parents, you can find Emily online on YouTube (youtube.com/@ebnmusic), Facebook (facebook.com/ebnmusic), Instagram @ebn.music, and TikTok @ebnmusic.

About the Illustrator

Malgorzata Detner is a Poland-based illustrator, born in 1989. She currently lives with her family, a cocker spaniel, snails, and two lovely rats in Warsaw. Her love of drawing began at a young age, influenced by her mother's paintings, but grew serious when she decided to pursue art in middle school. Although Malgorzata initially pursued a career in costume design with an interest in Victorian dresses, her daughter's birth made her return to traditional painting and digital illustration. Influenced by old animation, mysterious, fantastic worlds, animals, and creatures in vibrant colors are what she likes drawing the most. She draws digitally but also likes to incorporate hand-painted textures into her work. Malgorzata loves creating illustrations that remind her of childhood memories.

Parents, you can find her on Instagram @mdetner.illustration or at malgorzatadetner.com.